A SYMPHONY IN SAND

The Books in the
"Symphony" Trilogy:

A Requiem for Love
A Symphony in Sand
An Overture of Light

A SYMPHONY IN SAND

CALVIN MILLER

AUTHOR OF *THE SINGER* TRILOGY

WORD PUBLISHING
Dallas · London · Vancouver · Melbourne

A Symphony in Sand

Library of Congress Cataloging-in-Publication Data

Miller, Calvin
        A symphony in sand / by Calvin Miller
        p. cm.
        Second vol. in Symphony Trilogy
        ISBN 0-8499-0688-1
        1. Mary, Blessed Virgin, Saint—Fiction.   I. Title.
PS3563.I376S9 1990
813'.54—dc20   89-70766
                                CIP

Printed in the United States of America

0 1 2 3 9 AGF 9 8 7 6 5 4 3 2 1

A
SYMPHONY
IN SAND

Once in every universe
Some world is worry-torn
And hungry for a global lullaby.
O rest, poor race, and hurtle on through
     space—
God has umbilicaled Himself to straw,
Laid by His thunderbolts and learned
     to cry.

I

A solitary Child sat playing in the sun.
He lifted sand by chubby handfuls
Dropping it in gold cascades
That made the desert laugh.
His young and powerful guardian
Stood by, devouring Him in steadfast gaze.
At length, the tall man knelt
And reached out to the Child.
The Boy extended him
A grip of desert sand.
His guardian then took the dab of gold,
And poured it gently on the Infant's head.
Even as the sand fell desert-ward
The man's smile broke as sunlight
Erupting in pronouncement,
"Earthmaker, Glorious, be baptized
With the very earth You formed."
The gold trickled through his fingers
In showers of dancing diamonds,
That splashed upon the Child.

Above the man and Child
High rusted, ivied gates stretched upward.
The ancient doors were
Hinged to mossy granite.
Old hate-begotten grudges
Still seemed to cling in gray and green
To desolate and crumbling stones.

The towering man beneath the somber
        gates
Traded his light and lilting liturgy
For a vaulting and vivacious shout
That gobbled up the silence of the place,
"Live, Boy, till these old gates
Be shattered and sanctuary opens wide

To hold the wedding rites of God and
    humankind.
Live, I say, till every earthly desert
Repents its barren sands,
And gives birth unto a river.
Then shall all men lay by their swords
To gather holy rust
And laughing mothers hold their children
Unafraid of plague.
Grow manward, Boy,
Till hate at last smelts daggers
Into spoons and feeds its enemies. . .
Till tyrants give their dungeon keys
To priests and the blood-rich soil
Of battlefields grows grain
To feed the soldiers
Of a finer cause.
Grow older, Child, and as You grow,
The putrid halls of death shall change to healing
    rooms
Where sickness may meet sunlight.
Clap little hands till, wounded,
Your strong fingers shall
Strangle all the pointless causes
That eat up human hope.
Dance little feet until your injured footprints
Shall explode with fire enough to
Sear the wounds of violence
And every planet sings a better song!"

His rhapsodizing stopped at once!
He drew his sword.
"Declare yourself!"
He roared into the thick green shadows
That gathered in the stubby wood
Behind the wide-eyed Boy.
"The Child has come!
It is the Age of the Convergence!"

The word "convergence" floated heavily
Threading its way into a serpent's den.
The reptile woke!
Two yellow eyes snapped open.
Coral gold and black unbraided all in liquid
      movement
As he slithered into sun.
He fanned his neck,
Rearing, half-length, until his shadow
Fell across the Boy.

The Child was unafraid.

"So the Convergence comes at last!"
The reptile hissed.

"It does."

"And you've come here to these old walls
To announce this final shining age. . . ."

"I have!"

"What irony,
That His eternal fanfare should sound first
Here at the very gates
Where I defeated Him!
When last these old doors swung
There passed a man and woman,
Who traded innocence for knowledge
And found that they were gods,
Albeit, most unhappy gods!"
If serpents may be said to smirk,
The haughty cobra grinned at the Child.
"So this is Earthmaker!
Tell me, is He vision or reality?
As He is or shall be?"

"*Is* or *was* or *shall be*
Are but the piteous
Categories of those who have
So little time they must divide
It into then or now.
This Child is God made man,
And, as He *is* He *shall be*.
Earthmaker shall enwomb Himself in innocence,
Umbilical Himself to need,
Crying out at cold damp midnights,
Whimpering in dependency for human milk."

"Then this small thing which I behold
Is great Earthmaker in rehearsal to be man?"

"He needs no practice, Slithe,"
The man stared firmly into the reptile's eyes,
Whose gaze broke under his authority.
"The heaviness of glory
Demands His gentle form come slowly.
For Terra is an old woman now.
And spinning slow of age,
She wobbles in her palsied orbit.
Should all His vastness come too suddenly
On this uncertain world
His splendor would destroy it."

The serpent hissed a grinning joy.
"I'm glad He comes a Child
For children are an easy mark for evil.
I shall play about His cradle
And envenom all His dreams
Till dragons stalk His sleep."

The Child laughed and scooped
The sand and held it outward
To the serpent.

Ansond joined the Child in glee
Until their double laughter climbed the ivied walls,
"See, Slithe, He's unafraid!
He's armored by a kind of power
Your fangs can never pierce!"

"No power is so unwoundable!"

The golden man reached up with doubled fists,
Enraged by crass audacity,
"How naive is evil!
Behold the power of Holiness!
This aging world can never stand
Before the sway of purity!
His is the power of innocence
That grows from new, chaste love,
And holy inwardness.
This Child, unspoiled by power,
Can fear no serpent, hear no threat,
Or know no terror in the night!
Coil all around His cradle, if you will.
He will but stroke your head
With gentle hands
And bless you with the force of love
Born in His own unfearing eyes.
Innocence can sleep among the wolves
        untroubled.
It distills like dew
In sweetest sunrise
And plays untroubled in the maw of hell.
Innocence is deaf to thunder,
And made so rich by lavish trust
It never thinks of poverty.
For butterflies are gold
And rainbows are the emerald crowns
Of kings who never have learned fear.
It's innocence that gives the gracious wind its
        strength

And lifts the fragile flowers into the gales
And smiles at sifting petals."

"Sheer poetry, Ansond."
The serpent sneered
Then thickened to a man.
They quarreled, but
The Child who was between them
Played unaware of all their rhetoric.
"Ansond, you forget so soon our ancient grudge.
It burns no slower now than it did then
In the war of realms—
Where sword to sword we fought."

"No, Slithe, I could never
Let that horror slip from mind.
The universe itself recalls your blasphemy!
How painful yet the memory!
I begged you then to return to Him who gave
You being—You would not and lost all!"

"Not lost—but gained all!
This planet now is mine—this entire realm!
You've nothing, Ansond . . . nothing!"

"Wrong! Krystar!" Ansond
Used the serpent's older name—
"These I have!"
He tore his tunic off!
His bronzed chest was laced with silver scars!
"These, lost friend, are the marks of loyalty!
I bear each one in honor, and yet
My scars do not compare
With those this Child will one day wear!"

The World Hater stepped toward the Boy
And reached to Him as if to pick Him up!
Instantly, the gold man stepped between them

And in that single step was transformed to a lion.
The Hater shrank in terror,
Dwindling downward to a snake again.
In but a moment the old foes
Faced each other as lion unto cobra,
Power confronting power with fierce defiance.

The lion roared and circled
The still untroubled Child.
He nudged the Child with his broad nose,
And both of them walked slowly off.
Their substance thinned as they moved outward
Toward the fruitless plain,
Losing firmness even as they walked.
Their opaque blurs of vanishing reality
Dimmed to a haze that fled the cobra's straining
      eyes.

"So this was only an illusion.
There is no Child . . . no lion. . . !"
The cobra hissed into the desert air.
The desert chose to take the part of truth
And shouted in reply!
"The Age of the Convergence dawns.
Let every mountain range declare with joy
The lion roars and God is born a Boy."

A heavy crown
Can force the face of any weary king
Toward the ground.
But here and there wise kings
Bid crowns good-bye—
And find without their crowns
They're light enough to fly.

II

It was night, the time
When Melek most felt his years.
His queen was dead—long dead.
A decade of cool desert nights
Had come and gone since
She had slept that final sleep
Where waking is forbidden.
For as many nights he'd sat alone
Upon the balustrade
Of a palace he must soon leave kingless.

Melek knew the stars.
They were his friends—his only friends.
They understood his longings!
He ached for things that could not be
And wished he could restore the past . . .
If only one of his lost sons had lived!
But alas he had no child, no heir, no hope—
No kingdom and no king to follow him.
He stood and leaned far out
Above the cracked-tile roof.
"Loneliness numbs thought," he mused.
"And older sight sees only things
That clearly say they're here.
Poor eyes do not betray me.
Be either blind or honest.
For what I now see on the garden lawn
Defies all sense and yet forbids
Me look away."

A vision stopped his words:
A single Child
Sat playing in the starlight.
The Boy lifted up his head
And smiled so broadly that it seemed
His smile would gather all the fading light,

Then wash old Melek's vision black.
The aged sovereign rubbed his eyes and laughed
    aloud.
"Dead palace . . . empty courts.
How long since your gray walls
Have seen a Child?
Earthmaker, play no tricks on me.
I've lived alone too long.
Call yourself no God of mercy
If this Child be not real!"

His weary legs at once grew young!
His feet flew as though his
Queen were yet alive
And there to bless his coming.
Down, down, down,
And nimbly—too—he clipped
The steps from balcony to garden.
When he had turned past hedge
And wall, he cried aloud . . .
"The Child *is* here and He is *real!*
But stop . . . and slowly now . . ."
He checked his furious pace,
Lest his starving longing
Frighten the Child into devouring shadows.
Old and young they stared—
Eye to eye—each moved faceward
Toward the other.

With trembling hands the old one reached out first
    to touch . . .
To let his fingers test his vision.
His joyous touch approved his sight!
He gave a little cry!
The Child too reached out
Begging with His eyes.
Melek slipped his hands beneath the Boy's arms
And lifted Him.

Crushing the Child to his chest, he whispered,
"O let me die or never more awake!
My crown, my kingdom,
And all my fading years for this!"

The Boy laid his soft, small hand
Against the hard old face.
A long-forgotten joy welled up inside of Melek
As he felt the little fingers
Tangle in his old white beard.

A lion moved out of the shadows.
Melek might have frozen in his fear
Except a strong euphoria now wrapped his soul.
Transfixed in reverence, he worshiped,
Fearless in the wondrous night
Between a lion and a Child.

"Melek!" the voice seemed to come
From the beast born out of the shadows.
"This Child is yours in but a while.
Hold Him that His strength may come to you as
        bread.
Aged though you are,
You yet must make a journey.
It will be long and yet
True kings must spend themselves
In ways that their nobility demands.
Kiss the Boy . . .
Then set Him down and pray for strength
To bring your crown
And follow where the stars may lead.
The Child is yours . . .
But not until tomorrow."

The old king kissed the Child a final time,
But held to Him, refusing to release the joy.
"Now," Roared the lion, "Set Him down.

We only keep what we release.
We own by letting go!"

The old man set the Child down
And watched Him toddle toward the lion.
Together they walked into the shadows
And were gone.

"But where? When?" The old man asked.
No answer came.

The garden was as deserted as it had been
Throughout the empty years.
Melek's remorse stabbed at his aching reverie.
Funeral by funeral he'd felt this pain before
Till now, at last, his family was gone
And grief was all he had.
Grief—monstrous grief:
His meat, his drink,
His mocking mirror, his cold forbidding nights,
A decade of a table set for one.
He climbed the steps again,
Leaden . . . slow. His tired old limbs
Despised their heaviness.

When finally he reached the top
He looked into the heavens.
The stars were not his friends.
They were glittering deceivers—cheating him
With bright mirages—scalding all his dreams at
        midnights.
His eyes saw stars.
His mind, the vanished lion and the Child.
Suddenly he was seeing for the first time
What he had studied all his life.
The constellation of the lion in the high night dome!
His vision turned to the Constellation of the Child.
His face lit up at once!

He flew into his study, throwing
Star charts, all unsorted, to the floor.
What a night this was!
He was old and dying
When it first began.
Then came the Child and lion
And he was young until the vision died.
Then he was old again.
"But now," he wept in joy.
"I'm young all over!"
He held a parchment chart to the torchlight.

He flung it down upon the
Heavy table in the center of the room
And grabbed a quill and rule.
He dipped the pen in ink
And traced a line between the
Two great stars of second magnitude
As they appeared within the constellation of the
      lion.
He moved the quill to the opposite side
And drew a similar line between
The brightest stars in the Constellation of the
      Child.
He then extended those two lines until
They intersected near the center of the chart.
His eyes gathered tears in glinting torchlight
As he transcepted and arced the angles.
He shook his head and cried in self-rebuke:
"Melek! Never more call yourself
The friend of stars for you have
Lived in self-pity till it obscured your science.

"Grow young, old fool, the age of dark is past!
Convergence comes! You have an heir at last."

He walked to a large glass case
And reaching in, removed a crown.

He brought it to the marble table
And threw it down.
It settled like a spinning coin
In retiring echoes through
The dark corridors of his palace.
"Tomorrow I begin a joyous trek
To give my crown where star lines intersect."

Saints are never giants
Who hoped to do God favors.
They are only souls
Whose needs took root
In shallow dust,
Becoming redwoods grown
From dandelion spores.

III

The maid, Trouvere, came just at dusk
When sky was giving up its red.
Alone with lyre she came.
She set the thumb screws of her instrument
And played the separate strings.
When all the notes lay sweet and resonant
Upon the sea of gold, gray sand
She strummed them all at once and sang:

"Earthmaker,
Shall I, who am nothing,
Dare to tell You how I feel?
I must . . . I love You!
Your world is all so richly made
My eye can drink too little
Of the glory it beholds.
A butterfly is melody,
A hawk, a chorus of delight.
A tern against the blue
Sets free an entire symphony at night.
Is all of this for me?
The sand, the stars, the purple
Mountains gnawing at the fading sun
With jagged teeth of splendor?
O stop the seep of beauty
Now flowing into me or I shall burst,
Overfilled with ecstasy.

"O, Father Spirit,
I'm in love with You! In love!
How shall I speak?
I'm only poor Trouvere."

She laid aside the lyre
And growing silent, fell forward in the sand.
"O Father, Father!

I, orphan of the dark, can
Bear no sweeter word than this!
My song is far too small a trinket
To lay before Your splendor.
O how I need You!
My passions all are spirit-kindled.
I find no purpose in such
Trivial affections that some
Have named romance.
Your Holy flame makes small
The love of mortal hearts.
In such a fickle world
To try and name what earthly values matter most
Is but a fool's pursuit."

"I crave a love that will not let me go
When it has come to know me well.
I need a love so everlasting
It holds no course with unsure human promises.
I need You, O everlasting king!
If I may be of use to You
Then call me not Trouvere
But name me only by that need You have.
Make me a cup to bear Your drink,
A salver for Your meat,
Warmth for You if gods know cold,
A path for You, if gods need feet!
Whatever meager thing You ask,
Shall be my dignity.
Call me vessel unto honor.
Then I will not have breathed Your air in vain
Nor burdened Terra with a search
To find out why I lived."

Subdued by love
She noticed not that in the darkness
There passed behind her quietly
A Child and lion.

The stealthy beast looked with blazing eyes
Made warm with desert fire.
The Child spoke audibly a single word
Too softly for her searching soul to hear.
That word was "Mother," uttered infant clear.

In any desert, water may flow sweet—
Springing up in sandal prints of
wounded feet.

IV

The Artisan laid down his chisel
And turned to see Trouvere standing in the
    doorway of his shop.
"I'm glad you came, Trouvere."

He walked to her and took her hand
And they moved out into the early dusk.
"I'd hoped you'd come
And bring some resolution to my need.
Trouvere, we must decide
For time, like life itself, runs past us.
Will you marry me?
Please . . . I must know.
So often I have asked.
As long have you refused . . ."
He paused to cool
The urgency of issue
Lest he force her to an answer
He did *not* desire.
His urgency then melted into tenderness.
"Trouvere, I love you!"

"I wish you'd choose another word," She said.
"Let's talk of love some other time."

"Trouvere, is love an issue that can pick its time?
Can it learn the discipline of waiting?"

"O Artisan, if only you
Could understand the love I seek.
O that I understood it!
But this I swear,
There is a love not limited by lifetimes—
A noble love that shouts through the gales
Ordering brash thunderheads
To spend their roarings and begone!

And when the thunder dies
This love remains within
The conquering silence
That is the cowardly shadow of these
        retreating, whimpering storms!

"He is love—the only love which matters.
If I blot Him out, then madness rules.
But when I open up my window
Just a crack at midnight
The light of His celestial presence
Fills my room with majesty.
It's then I crave the whole of Him,
Not part or half a plate.
I must devour His love entire."
As she spoke she saw the hurt
Behind his eyes.

"Forgive me for I would not
Wound you with these words.
It's just that
My reason's eye is blinded by His nearness.
He is my treasure and my need,
A stream across the ashen wilderness
Of all my failures—
A bridge across
The chasms of my doubt."

The Artisan stopped her words and drew her close.

"Trouvere, another sort of love has brought us to
        this moment.
Can you not love both me and Him?"

He drew her even closer.
It seemed he felt her shudder in his arms.
"See," he said at last,
"Doubt hangs a heavy shadow over all our days.

Some strange and dark impending
Nudges me from sleep to fear
Like an advancing army I cannot define.
Some iron wedge like the one I sometimes use
To split a stubborn trunk of wood—
Is being driven even now between us.
Nightmares wake me
And I shake my fist into the vacant air
Above my bed and order
Leering demons from my room
As inwardly I tremble.
Love Him, but love me too!
Could He who owns the universe
Be jealous of my tiny need?
If *I* share you with Him
Can He be stingy in *His* recompense?"

He stopped and thrust at her a parcel of coarse
        cloth.
It was a loaf of bread.
Famine made his abrupt gift
An acceptable interruption
To their probing trysts of heart.

"Where did you . . ." She asked
Not finishing her question.

"Trouvere, the whole world isn't desert.
Every caravan bears treasures
And bread comes sometimes from the
        cunning.
I'd find you bread and grain to spare
If only . . ."

"It's just that it has been so long,
Since I have seen a whole loaf."
She threw herself into his arms
As though he'd given her a cask of jewels.

The desert had not yielded many treasures,
Like the loaf she held.

"They say this is the century
That Terra's sand will hold
Earthmaker's footprints."
Her statement followed nothing and preceded
      nothing.
She touched the bread and gazed out pensively.
Her eyes seemed empty as the sand.

The silence lingered, isolating in its quiet
All her wistful prophecy.

"It is theology," he said at last.
"Leave it with the temple graybeards or all its
      emptiness
Will make you empty too. Here is life . . ."
His large firm hand fell warm upon her own.
He kissed her.
She turned away and pointed to the thousand
      stars
That laughed at them as pricks of light,
Now wheedling a brilliant uproar in the
      desert sky.
"Behind those stars is life," she said.

"Trouvere, the other side of stars
Is Earthmaker's side.
This side is ours."
He left off argument.

She shrugged,
"Still, Earthmaker's not content to live so darkly
      distant
On the unseen side of any star wall.
O Artisan, do you not feel Him in the air?
His rich love richly begs my heart to sit in silence."

"But why?" he asked,
"How much silence?"

"Enough to hear the joy! The promise!
It floats around us even now.
It swims this sand in maddening intrigue
With rapture as could cleanse a world's fatigue.
Earthmaker lives! His century has come.
There shall be love enough to strike us dumb."

"Now we shall try your sweet
       communion vows
With single cup," the leper said.
"Give me your chalice first,
Then drink yourself.
But courage—for
The last three priests
Looked at my eroded face
And left their sweet religious cup
       and fled.
I later sipped their living wine—
       it tasted dead!"

V

Sand swirled across the sickly dunes!
The plague had come!
Mothers buried sons by husbands,
Lovers grieved new graves
Then walked alone.
Day by day the death carts came.
Hooded criers walked on either side
Of flat-slab wheels and moaned,
"Bring out your dead!"

Old Imperius heard their wail
As they passed by. He too was sick,
But welcomed death,
For his entire family was gone—devoured by
        plague.
He knew he soon must take *his* turn upon the
        tumbrel.
Fever gnawed at him with burning breath.
He shuddered in its wrenching spasms
As down the road the carter's cry
Grew soft with distance,
"Bring out your dead, none but the dead are free!"

He lit a candle, opened up an ancient book and
        read.

His lips moved slowly as his fevered
        eyes picked up the words.
"Blessed be the Maker of all worlds!
He saves all those who walk within the
        counsel of His love."

He paused and looked away then read—again,
"He is our help in every trial,
Watching us as eagles guard their young
In craggy nests above the storms."

Imperius' faint voice threaded
Through the weathered shutters.
"Earthmaker, I am dying, and I can bear it—
But alone?—like this?
I am not afraid of death,
But, O I am ashamed!
Human beings in times of plague,
Cast off their God-like dignity
To climb on carts of corpses."

His fever once more chilled him.

He shuddered then and fell in weakness
Knocking both his book and candle from the stand.
The falling book released a lock of golden hair.
Imperius held it to the light and cried,
"Emma, O Emma, were you ever in my life?
Am I insanely dreaming to recall
That I once held you dressed in wedding white?"

"Then we had passions, yes, and plans.
And then the years . . . the years . . . the years!
But Emma, when I held you in your final sickness
And you shuddered in those agonies I could not
        kiss away,
I cursed Earthmaker,
For my mind was webbed with hurt.
They made me lift you to the cart.
I would have buried you, my darling,
In the wild flowers of the high plateaus,
But no, it had to be in death's gray cloth!
I tried to tell myself that your death cart was the
        grand carriage of a queen.
But as it rumbled off,
I could not tell which shroud was yours.
O Emma . . . the fire came then . . . and
        now . . .
Tomorrow I will join you in the final silence.

Then Emma and Imperius shall
Be a common testament
That life's the grim report
That God is cruel and knows
No gracious news to bear mankind."

He paused a moment and
Pulled his rags about him.
"Earthmaker, are You but
The mocking, last estate of old men
Who worship healthy gods
Who've never faced the plague?"

His sickness came so hard upon him now,
He could no longer speak.
His burning fever ignited a delirium so lovely
It charmed him at the brink of death.
There stood a lion and a Child before him.

"You look too high for God, Imperius,"
The lion roared.
"He's coming unto Terra even now.
And this, Imperius, is He."
The lion nudged the Boy.
"You are wrong to think Earthmaker
Lives in realms which never can know pain.
As this Child grows He will become
A man susceptible to plague.
He, like you, will face the loneliness of dying.
And deal with all you've faced.
I give to you this promise as a gift:
You shall not die till you have met this Child."

The lion walked up to the trembling, dying man.
His giant muzzle fell full across the old and hopeless
     face.
Imperius, trembling at the lion's size,
Made one small groaning utterance.

He fell unconscious
And slept as children
Sleep on summer afternoons.
The vision died and then his fever.

But not Imperius!
He lived and read the book.
When anybody asked how he'd survived the plague
He smiled and said,
"I have one last appointment.
I dare not die till it be kept.
Convergence comes—Earthmaker learns to beg.
He'll dress in flesh to cure our world of plague."

What we know here is barely sanity.
What we own here amounts to vanity.
God sets before all men but one grand,
Worthy cup—
HOPE.

VI

M other . . ." called a Child entreatingly.
The voice sounded as though it were just
     beyond the door
That opened on the narrow empty street.

Trouvere drew her shawl about her
And opened up the door.
Curiosity . . . drew her into dusk.
The silver light cast mauve shadows
Over purple cobblestones that wore a sheen
Of furious compulsion.
She tightened her eyes to make them see
All that might be hiding in the beckoning
     shadows.
There was nothing!

She then turned back inside,
Convinced the dusky streets
Held but the whispering echoes
Of children who had played there
In the glaring light of noon.
She lifted up the latch
To enter her small house again.

"Mother," once more came
The beckoning and plaintive word
From further down the haunted lane.
"Some Child *is* there . . ."
She thought as she walked into the night.

She reached at last the shadowed wall
And squinted into darkness.
Suddenly she saw a little form
Eclipse the bold veridian sky.
"Please wait . . ." Trouvere cried
To the shadowed blur of childhood

That hurried her to walk and then to run
In an attempt to catch the tiny silhouette.
And so she found herself
Chasing plaintive echoes
To the desert's silver edge.

"Mother . . ." finally the sound took shape!
There was a Child!
She saw Him clearly now, reaching out to her.
But as she moved toward Him He retreated.

"Please . . . I'll take You home!
Come . . . don't be afraid!"
With reluctance then the Child came forward
      slowly.
They reached out to each other
Tentatively . . . fearfully . . . hopefully,
Till at last their hands touched!
And then Trouvere picked up the Child.

"You're a long way from home, little one!"
Trouvere brushed His flaxen hair aside.

"A long . . . long way . . ."
She heard a voice behind her
And wheeled to see a man
Whose skin and clothing were as lustrous
As any gold ever mined on Terra.
She was afraid, yet the man did nothing
That would startle her.
"This Child, reality unborn,
Is your own Son . . . but not yet!
He speaks now that one word
Earthmaker must rehearse . . . Mother!"

He paused, then turned to her,
"Sit here, Trouvere,"
He gestured toward a solitary rock.

"I'll tell you of a miracle that's vast
And tiny all at once."

Trouvere sat down!
The gold-skinned man continued.
The Boy that she held
Patted her face even as he talked.

"The Father-Spirit loves with a passion
Gathered from its wide galactic essence
Out of the empty valleys of far distant worlds.
His love sweeps up its zeal from all the blazing light
Of stars, your eyes will never see.
And having gathered up the fullness of His
       universal being
He pours it now into this small
Dependent bit of flesh
That's nestled in your lap."

"Mother . . ." the Child said once again.

Ansond went on.
"Trouvere, meet Earthmaker!"

"But I don't understand!"

"It doesn't matter that you understand!
The strength of all Earthmaker's logic
Always meets the human mind as madness."

"The Father Spirit grieved the day
He closed the gates of Sanctuary
And shut the first man and woman
From the shelter of His love.
Since that day, He's known no hunger
But the one that grieves their absence.
He wants them back, Trouvere, as lovers
Of each other and Himself.

So He is coming!
Not in the regal splendor of His distant glory,
But in this small reduction that you hold!"

Trouvere was suddenly afraid.

"I'm mad!" she cried. "My love for Him
Has snatched my mind away!"
She sat the Baby on the ground and stood.
"You are not there . . . not there!" She shouted
At the Child.
The Child looked hurt.
Her heart reached out to Him.
She wished she'd not denied Him
Yet she must not weaken in her resolve
Or the world would call her mad.
She wheeled and walked away!

She turned back only once and looked.
The man, made small by distance,
Seemed to be stooping toward the Child.
Then there was no man,
Only a great beast
Whose burning feral eyes stared after her.
The lion roared.
She fled into the night.
"I must not speak a word of all I've seen
Lest He who fathers reason seem obscene."

Darkness is a cloak
That dresses imps in angel robes.

VII

The Artisan walked slowly
Through the same dark night
That had left Trouvere so troubled.
A stranger silently appeared
And walked in perfect stride beside him.

"The maid you love
Has slept with me . . ."
The villain's knife-edged words
Were out at once,
And thrust their blade of
Accusation quietly
Into his peace.

The stunned Artisan turned
And faced his love's accuser.
"What can you mean?"
He charged.
Even in the stingy light
The craftsman saw that the stranger's eyes
Were yellow-lit as if by hell.

The unwelcome intruder smirked,
"Here is the spoiling of your
Long-awaited bridal night."
He pointed to his own loins.
"Craftsman-to-be-pitied,
I have already been where you have only
Dreamed of being
When all your faithless vows are spoken.
Deluded lover!
Your maid is false as Hell itself!"

In hot and instant anger
The Artisan doubled his firm hand into a heavy fist
And thrust it forward toward the mocking eyes.

The grinning face dissolved!
His flying fist met nothing!

His fiend accuser melted.
All was silent!
The carpenter doubted first the silence,
Then his senses.

"Liar!" He shouted to the empty gloom
Where Trouvere's false accuser
Had so lately fanged the darkness.
"You've come either from my troubled mind,
Or from the gates of Hell
And I trust neither source.
All evil seeds can bear but evil fruit
When men trust demons peddling lies as truth."

"I think that God has given me a task!"
"Was the task an easy one?"
"It was and O so sweet!"
Then it was not from God,
For what He asks
Requires the rending of the soul.

VIII

A phantom hulk moved in her room!
Trouvere awoke, afraid.
A pair of eyes made luminous as glinting
     amber stared through her soul.
And yet the eyes were somehow generous
     lanterns, warmly lit.

"Who are you?" Trouvere asked.
She was answered only by the breathing
Of a beast which walked to her in darkness
And with his muzzle, nudged her from the bed.
She rose and dressed and followed.

Out, out, they moved through lane and street . . .
A woman and a lion,
Walking silently at midnight
Like innocence and power
By grace betrothed.

They came to Trouvere's desert place,
Where she had last seen
Both the Child and the lion.

The lion roared and reared himself on powerful
     haunches
And instantly became the golden man.

"Where is the Child?"
Trouvere seemed most insistent.

"There is no Child—not yet!
What you beheld was but Earthmaker's promise."

"But I held Him and He touched me and He
     spoke!"

"Majestic truths declare themselves
Before they come to be!"

At his words, Trouvere covered both her ears
And looked up to the heavens begging "NO!
I can no longer bear this madness!"

"Earthmaker needs a window,
An opening where Spirit may pass
With power in such abundance
That those who say
He is remote
And comfortable in sky,
May repent of their resentments.
Are you resolved to be
The window of His love?"

"Will His love be kind?"

"Kindness may seem brutal in its grace.
As when a surgeon cuts at death to offer life.
But the scars of love display
The hope that grows from pain."

The golden man went on,
"But pain does not mark only human
        suffering.
With every lesion you wear,
Earthmaker, too, will bleed,
With sky-sized wounds and agonies.
Trouvere, it is an honor to be chosen.
From all of Terra's women
This grace has come to you!
In you two very different worlds will touch
To keep each separate realm
From that poor arrogance which says,
'MY WORLD IS ALL THERE IS.'"

He gestured to the sky.
"There," he rumbled, low of voice,
"Is where Earthmaker and His Son now live.
His Son will soon walk Terra sands,
But as He now is, He cannot walk."

"And why not as He is?"

"He has no flesh and blood, and
Without these poor habiliments
He cannot stand as being
Fashioned on this planet."

"No flesh or blood!"
Trouvere voiced her brusque objections,
"How then fleshless, bloodless can He be?"

"Trouvere, Trouvere.
Let God be larger
Than your understanding!
Indeed His Son is now so vast in size
That all these distant starfields you behold
Would fit into the sparkle of His Father's eye.
Yet soon He will reduce Himself
To mortal form and size.
For greatness needs a way
To enter little worlds."

"A window?" Trouvere's mind was stretching.

"Window . . . or door . . . yes . . .
Some bridge where vastness
May change realms
And make poor Terra understand
That flesh and blood are but weak replicas
Of being in its greatest form.
His coming will overshadow you with inner life.

I've nothing more to say but 'wait' and 'yield.'
Clutch these two words unto your soul."

Ansond melted into night.
Trouvere found herself alone.
"I'm mad!" she cried,
"Earthmaker, torture me no more.
I beg You!
Do not ask this forfeiture of mind.
From such delusions can I mother God?
No! Never! Never!
The wombs beneath such troubled minds
Bear murderers not kings and gods.

"Am I too frail to hold the honor that is mine?
If infant men may bring their mothers infant woes,
What sort of pain may infant Gods produce?
I won't be vessel to immortal schemes
My weakness cannot bear such heavy dreams."

Some tribesmen still believe all lion
    cubs are stillborn
And cannot live until their sire
Breathes in their nostrils, waking them
    to life.
In such a way
Eden grows in savage souls.

IX

Trouvere dreamed and in her misty mind
She walked across a barren desert-scape
Until she met the lion.
Dropping to her knees before the beast,
With reaching hands she held his giant head
And stared into his tawny face.
A glint of starlight, like a desert diamond,
Gleamed in the beastly eye.
In that same lion's eye
She saw a mirror scene—An aged king,
Stumbling through a desert storm,
Shielding his face from cutting sands.
One of his thin arms ran through a coronet of gold
And the other ended in a hand that gathered
His hood tightly around his throat.

The old king stopped at length
And turned his back.
"As my name is Melek,
I never will be conquered;
I will live and see this Child, whose kingdom shall
Make one of two.
Whose very being shall unite all life."

He said nothing else, but turned into the wind
And walked.

Trouvere repeated the name he'd given to the
        wind,
"Melek, bear on, old one, somehow I know we'll
        meet.
Earthmaker," she said in reverence,
"Protect this patriarch."

She released the lion's head and sang
Unto the beast,

"Glint in this lion's eye, guide Melek's feet!
Illumine all his wilderness tonight.
Old kings give up their crowns reluctantly.
Dim eyes beg sight and cling to dying light."

"Do lions cry with grieving sighs that rise
As stars in lion's eyes? Take leave of me!
Hold not your place in this small ordered sea.
I give you up! Roar elsewhere and be free."

"Stalk him, great beast, lest he should ever doubt.
Roar through the winds and tempest as you may.
His ebbing mind needs find a guardian.
He'll die without a lion in the way."

The night dissolved.
Trouvere's singing folded into mist,
The fire-eyed beast was gone.

Hundreds of miles eastward across the desert
Melek struggled on against the winds.
His stamina was nearly gone.
He fell in sand that the wind
Whipped into devouring cruelty.
On his knees . . . to the wind
He felt a sudden reprieve in the deadly air,
As if some form had come between him
And the storm's ferocity.
He turned to see the lion he had first seen
In the Palace Garden.
"You are the sign," he whispered to the beast.
"We are both kings. How odd we both should
        meet.
Perhaps we'll lay our crowns at better feet."

A dying child gives life up willingly,
If he is loved and held while dying.
Triumphant innocence can smile upon
Such terrors as make gladiators scream.

X

From time to time Imperius would talk
With the small Child promised
By the golden man.
The Child existed
Only in his deepest longing.
"Dear little one . . . the world is sick.
The plague walks with heavy boots
That gouge the earth with graves.
The night my Emma died she knocked a
Jar of water to the floor,
And even as the water flowed away
Her life ebbed, too.
I studied all the shards of glass that shattered
Round her bed like broken bits of life."

"But enough! I speak but to myself,
And wait for You.
Run along now . . ."

He imagined the Boy walking off.

Thus, the Child of Promise came and went
Keeping all his loneliness at bay
Until the glorious day should come.
"O Infant Grand, I bless Your fragile coming
And before I join my Emma
I'll yet reach out to lift You to my breast
And close my life with joy.
Death, you can no longer paralyze.
The Child-God comes, till then my spirit flies."

Adam's ghost walked through
     Hiroshima's ruins
Giving apples to the dying,
Begging their forgiveness.

XI

On that same night when
The desert solstice was born
Ansond, leaving off his lion form, came once
    again.
His presence did not frighten Trouvere now,
Nor did she draw away in fear.
"All argument is gone—
I am Earthmaker's window,"
She said softly.

"And can you live with pain?"
Ansond inquired.

"I do not relish pain,
But, I shall steel myself
To bear it as I can."

Ansond smiled and vanished in a swirl of light.
The path of fire
That followed him to nothingness
Gathered itself in brilliant incandescence
That spiraled upward, reversed its course,
Then bore down as wild determined flame
Enveloping her now willing soul
And wrapping her compliance
In conceiving fire.

When Trouvere could no longer
Stand the brilliance
She fell unconscious.
Miracle and love were one at once.
Spirit-life took root in clay.
The fire passed and Trouvere slept!
And as she did, a vision
Unfolded in the dying fire.
A man and woman,

Bent by age and great despair,
Walked to her sleeping form.
The Matriarch reached down,
And touching Trouvere's hair, wept.

"You, child of yielded spirit,
Will serve Him better far than I once
      served.
I wanted knowledge, yes, and power.
I wanted disobedience to make me wise,
And thus devouring the forbidden
I changed His paradise to Hell,
And cursed the streams of Sanctuary
To call myself 'like God!'
See what a scourge is laid
Upon my disobedience.
I loved the serpent more than He
Who woke me on a summer day in Paradise."

"Don't talk this way, woman from my side!"
The old man grieved to see her crying.
"Dearest love," she said,
"You know it is true!
I cursed it all, and worse, I then cursed you.
Yes, you the most of all.
I could cry a requiem for
Sanctuary, if by my tears
I could undo the misery I've done."

"No . . . no!" he cried. "You take
Too much upon yourself."
He drew her near.
"My sin is mine . . ."
His words died.
Silence reigned.

"She is beautiful, isn't she?"
The woman said at last,

Gesturing to Trouvere, sleeping still beneath
The thinning light streams.

"She is as you are . . . beautiful!"
The old man said.

"As I *was?*"

"You are!" He insisted.
"Do you think that beauty ever lies
In youth or perfect features?
Tonight our double sin is healed.
Within this maid is Sanctuary born again."

"O Trouvere, how blessed you are!"
The woman cried exulting.
"I gave birth to quarreling sons,
Whose egotism, like my own,
Only spoiled all the earth it touched.
Reverse my ruin!
Live and give life!
Earthmaker's Son and song unsung
Is sleeping now
In this small, yet glorious space,
The world calls Blessed.
Two women are we here
Whose trust and lack of trust
Stabbed and made alive
The destiny of every soul.
Blessed, too, is He who sleeps within you!
He'll rise to smash the hated gates
I closed on human hope."

"Come away." The old man took her arm.
Drawn by her man, the woman walked
          away
With steps made light with hope.

In a final, and lingering glance,
She turned and wept,
"Live, child of earth, to bear the Child of sky.
Give Terra life that's unafraid to die."

The world lies lost without restraint
When gigolos kneel down with saints.

XII

The Artisan had made the matter firm.
The marriage date would be
In six short months—
So brief and yet so long a time!
On his way to see his maid,
The accusing stranger came again.

"Surprised to see me in the daylight?"
The hooded man rejoined.
Those were the very words
The Artisan had framed within his mind.
A rasping voice emerged from underneath the
        hood.
If words can be said to coil as serpents do,
His words came
Twisted—adder like,
"Nightly now, I'm sleeping with your maid.
Odd, isn't it, that one man's future hopes
Are but the spent reality of other men's past
        appetites.
Forbidden treats are ever best."

"Liar!" The craftsman ground the whispered word
        between his teeth.
Gurgling laughter issued
From the shaded face.

The stranger's hood was brown
But filigreed with silver threads
That twisted in metallic cobras,
Coiled, and entwined among
Emblazoned leaves of gold,
That rose from copper apples
And other kinds of pale, embroidered fruit.
The curious evil needlework
Intrigued the Artisan.

"You like the silver-threaded hood?"

The Artisan walked unanswering.
The stranger turned his head enough
To let the sunlight catch the high cheekbones
Beneath the canopy of brown brocade.
The glancing light flew upward to his eyes,
Which, like the stranger's words, seemed evil,
Slitted, old,
As though they'd yellowed
With a thousand centuries of staring hate.
The hood fell back.
The man-thing laughed, and tossed his head
In arrogance, then grinned and disappeared.

The Artisan was troubled.
His hallucinations came too often,
And seemed too real to doubt.
This hideous demon
Had twice accused his own beloved.
He trusted his Trouvere and yet . . .

"O Trouvere, Trouvere!" He said half-aloud
As he continued down the narrow lane.
"I betray you in my heart by my unwilling
Remembrance of this liar's vile eruptions."

He stopped his mumbling and tried
To walk past all his fears,
But froze as he beheld a cobra,
Black as gliding ebony, race past him.
The venomous creature stopped
At a distance in the dirt ahead.

The serpent twisted its sleek body
Into a triple circle, then
Lifting its wide head, glided quietly away.

The lovers met,
Some distance from Trouvere's small home.
"O Trouvere—I'm tormented
By visions that my mind cannot lay by.
Evil walks with me.
It interrupts my sleep
And tells me lies too hideous for you to bear!"

"Dear Artisan, I too
Am stalked by visions
Of a lion in the night."

"What can you mean a 'lion in the night'?"

"I dare not tell you
What I mean,
I must not try . . . only trust me—
Indeed let us both trust.
I'll trust the giver of my vision
And you trust me and wait."

"How long to wait to trust?"

"A little while . . . a little while . . ."

"A little while," he looked away.
Tears filled his repetition of her words.
They embraced, as somewhere in the weeds
Beside the road a reptile hissed in sighs,
Grinned over fangs and watched through jaundiced
        eyes.

They say that eighty fathoms under
    earth is Hell.
Believe it not!
It lies in shallow flesh—
Three inches underneath the chest.
There jealousy may dwell.
Dwell, nay, not merely dwell,
But writhe and sting itself to death.

XIII

When they approached the stoop
Of Trouvere's home
There lay upon a boulder there
Beside her door,
A brown cloak, sewn with silver filigree.

"Trouvere, where did you get this?"
The Artisan demanded, grabbing at the cloak.

"Nowhere. I got it nowhere.
I don't know how it got there
Nor whose it is." She rambled.

The Artisan's doubts grew fangs
As real as those that marked
The hooded being of his all-elusive foe.
He turned in silence, only for a moment,
Then wheeled and nearly shouted:
"Trouvere! My heart is torn!
I've met a man who says that he . . ."

"Yes?" She gave a single word and waited.

"This cloak . . . again . . . whose?"

This time he spoke so loudly
Her tears no longer stopped behind her eyes.
The carpenter beheld her tears,
But saw them as admission.

He threw the broadcloth to the ground.
As his anger faded to remorse,
He softened his denunciation,
"Trouvere, I never gave you cause . . ."

"O Artisan, your words are knifelike.
They swarm at me like murderous assassins.

I can't know all that troubles you,
Still I can see a gray doubt in those eyes
Which once beheld my face in love.
O beware the demon, Jealousy!
This devil wrecks the excellence of all relationships.
Jealousy's a libertine that sleeps in unclean beds
Conceiving other hungry imps that breathe
      suspicion.
He nibbles first at older promises
And then devours all future hope of
Seeing love restored.
He sometimes teaches martyrs
To despise their faith
And then delivers them
To nothing more than faithless living.
Scorn, love, his bitter doubt
Lest doubt's rehearsal
Form in you a bitter heart.
The hardest lies which we must circumvent
Are those our troubled, unsure hearts invent."

Motherhood's second heaviest burden is
That her children be compelled to watch
 her die.
Her heaviest burden is to be compelled
 to watch them die.

XIV

Trouvere's estrangement from her Artisan
Left her in sleeplessness
And set her wandering.
She heard a muffled sobbing as she
Passed a shaded section of the wall at evening.
She turned to see a woman huddled,
Weeping, with her head bent low,
Almost between her knees.
"Why do you weep?" Trouvere asked.

The woman, never looking up, replied,
"Please, go away!"
Trouvere wanted to comply, but
An aching that would not let her go
Prohibited her leaving.
She sat until the woman's grief seemed
Less violent, then she asked, "Are you alone?"
She felt ashamed to ask so obvious a question.
She was alone and her cutting grief
Further isolated her from any who might care.

The woman continued looking down,
Her tear-streaked face stared into dust.
"I have just come from the city!"
She stopped and let the silence rule.
"Yes . . . ?" Trouvere urged.

"My only son was executed there,
And I beheld him die," The woman said.
"Have you children?" The huddled being asked
The question muffled by her buried face.

"I shall have," replied Trouvere.

"I remember when my son was born . . ."
She paused again as though her frail tongue

Could not support the leaden words.
"I held him close and loved him for his helplessness
        and need.
That memory shall never leave
For today I watched him die.
No man can die a man
While any mother's there to see.
He died a little boy! A child who needed me!
And hurting were his eyes
As when he was a boy!

"He spoke but one word, 'Mother.'
His was not a man's voice,
Nor was his pain a man's pain.
He was a boy crying out to me,
Somehow as he did
When once he scraped a knee or
Felt a fishhook tear his infant hand.
I knew what to do back then.
Today I did not know."

"Executed and so publicly . . . that's the part
I barely could withstand.
His dying was so observed.
I begged the gawking world
To turn their eyes away in mercy.
For there are times when merely looking is a crime,
When our hurt should have the chance to hide
From eyes whose staring but enlarge our wounds."

"So at his dying place
I would not look at him
And add the pain of my own scrutiny."
She was silent for a moment,
Then went on.

"When he was but a little boy
I used to hold him near and think

How much he'd grown and how heavy he'd
     become
With the passing of each day.
Too soon the time came when
It grew difficult just to lift
Him into bed for naps.
Then once when we were dancing at the festival
He scooped me in his arms and held me
And I was most embarrassed.
But young men are so prone
To show the world their strength.
And yet I thought, it's right
For sons to carry parents
And hold them as a symbol.
For when he lifted me,
I saw the end of his dependence.
I knew the days would come
As surely as my years advanced;
I'd be infirm or invalid
And then my strong young son would carry me
As I had done for him."

Pausing for a moment she shrugged her shoulders
As if to escape the weight of all that she had seen.
"It was strange today when they took him from
His dying place, I leaned against his gallows
And they placed him in my arms.
I begged them do it and they did!
O he was light! I was so surprised!
I'd never held him as a man
And he was light . . . light!
I looked at him, remembering,
That long-ago dance festival.
I thought, if I could only hold him up
And dance him back to life,
I'd leave us laughing at his death.
I would unwrap the stillness

That twisted 'round his youthful smiling face
And he would live.

I held his wounded head a final time
And wept and said, 'O son!
Think not this furious turn of circumstance
Could ever turn me from the obligations of my
    motherhood.
I held you when you took your first, new breath.
I hold you now beyond all final need of breath.'
I kissed him then and called him 'sonny.'
It was not his name
And yet the name I'd always called him
When he fell asleep upon my lap.
'Sleep, sonny, for this world did not deserve your
    presence.'"

Silence!

Trouvere at last reached boldly out to her
And raised the woman's face toward her own.

The faces were identical!
The woman was herself!
Her blazing, tear-washed eyes
Cut visions like a sword through Trouvere's soul.
And as Trouvere stared into her own suffering eyes
The woman's solidarity gave way.
She melted into air leaving Trouvere
Stunned and alone.
Still reaching to her crushed, inner self,
She turned her ashen, frightened face to the sky:
"Such shadows alter hope . . . . Hold time in sway.
Die now, dead eyes, lest you behold that day!"

"Look, Saint, I'm a God made warm
    by love,"
Said a devil impersonating deity.
"I believe you," cried the Saint.
"May I see the scars you spent in
    loving me?"
"I have no scars!"
"Then you're no God! Nor do
    you love!"

XV

The outside air was cool
Enough to let her fevered mind
Hold counsel with itself.
Weeks now had gone,
Her Artisan had not come.
Trouvere looked down at herself,
Convinced she could no longer hide
What she must make her world believe.
She'd once seen a woman executed for
        adultery
And the vision of the martyred woman
Would not leave her mind.
She heard again, and even yet again
The felted thumping of the stones.
Even now she felt a stinging in her eyes—
The burning heat that told her
Should she herself face such a crowd
She would not beg for life.
Still, doubts, like arrow volleys, flew at her.
Could she be mad? Could her vanished night
        of glory
Have been an hallucination of such strength
That she, herself, believed it?
Her mind seemed firm and yet she knew
That those most mad were
The last ones to suspect their madness.

"Earthmaker!" She cried. "I need You still
To separate bright reason from insanity."

Suddenly, the sky burst with a
Floating fleck of light
That doubled all its silver
Into gold and settled at her feet.

A lion roared.

"Trouvere, you are the chosen window,"
Ansond stepped out of glistening shafts of light.
"The season of your trial by fire has come.
Now you must hold to truth
While others call it false.
Friends, relatives—your only love will soon
Lament your broken mind.
Some will threaten you
With stoning and with death,
But do not fear!
You *are* Earthmaker's Chosen!"
He touched her once again,
Then lionized himself,
And leapt into invisibility.

Trouvere shouted to the sky which swallowed him.
"Earthmaker! Terra is a needy place,
I'll spend the coins of trust to purchase grace."

The lips know only shallow tunes.
The heart is where great symphonies
are born.

XVI

Imperius would wake and wonder at his gift
    of life.
The plague that came as shrouded horror
Had now abandoned every street
And while the living were not many
Imperius rose each day to bless the sun
And remind himself that every meaningful breath
Of life was given to some purpose.
His purpose was to wait!
He waited for a Baby.
But where he and the Child would meet
Was as much a mystery
As his return from that murky land of near-death.

He still talked
With the Child he oft imagined.
Indeed his dreams were filled with children!
And thus he slept the sound sleep
Of those whose confidence was locked
Away in vaults on other worlds that
Never had known thieves or threats.

One night, however, his sleep unfolded
In a vision so majestic he woke up
In another time.
At last he understood the Glory
Of his waiting for a little Child
For he saw the man the Child would become.
The Child-made-man was tall with eyes that
    pierced the gloom.
And yet those eyes absorbed
All pain and hurt and cleaned the wounds
Of lepers just by looking on them.

The Child-made-man walked forth into the streets
And passed His shadow over thronged cities.

He passed a crumpled soul wrapped in self-pity,
Begging by a wall.
"Why do you beg?" the Child-man asked.
"I must beg to live," the beggar answered.
"My feet are only useless clubs that will
Not carry me."

"Look on Me, My name is Liberty!" the Child-man
    cried.
The beggar looked.
His useless feet were suddenly made strong.
He rose upward, steadied himself
Against the nearby wall
And then walked . . . made whole by joy!
The Child-man smiled and in that instant fell.
His feet were now just stiffened clubs
On which He could not walk.
The beggar's gnarled crutches lay yet upon the
    ground.
He now used them to pull Himself upward
And hobble slowly down the lane.
"I am Liberty," He said, "Made swift by beggar's
    crutches!"

He walked on through the dreaming mists
Of human misery until at last
He met a youth whose face was torn by scars.
Her weeping made His soul reach out.
"Why do you cry?" He asked.
"Can You not see?" she replied.
"I fell into fire when but a child and
Now my disfigurement is but
A mask of ugliness that forbids all hope
Of living in a secure world made warm with
    friendship."

"Look on Me . . . My name is Hope!" the
    Child-man commanded.

She looked and as she gazed
Her scars gradually sunk in new soft skin
But broke like ugly calluses of hate on His own face.
As her countenance became clean and young and
    beautiful
The Child-man, in that moment, was born a thing
    grotesque.
She ran off into the distance
And her joy was wondrous great
But not as great as His.
He leaned hard on His crutch and through a
Face made ugly by His own desiring
He cried after her in joy.
"I am Hope, made beautiful by craving ugliness.
I am Liberty, made swift by beggar's crutches."
He sang and hobbled slowly up a long, defiant hill.

In but a while, the Child-man came across
An old man shivering in the cold shadows of early
    evening.
He was naked and the night would soon steal his
    life.

"Have you no coat?"
The Child-man asked.

"I had one but it was stolen."

"Look on Me! My name is Love!"
He twisted from His own coat
And gave it to the man.
His giving left Him nearly naked
And unprotected in the night.
The man who had received His coat
Walked out into streets, made warm by knowing
His nights would be endurable.
The Child-man smiled!

"I am Love, made warm by nakedness.
I am Hope, made beautiful by craving ugliness.
I am Liberty, made swift by beggar's crutches."

At last His hobbling brought Him
Through a thousand sunsets and vast fields of
        misery.
He stopped and shuddered at what lay before Him.
He grimaced as He faced a distant hill.
For there He saw three gallows.
He hobbled to their center.
His eyes were filled with tears.
For on the first gallows He saw the man
Whose feet He'd taken as His own.

"Did You but make me strong to let me die?"
The dying man confronted Him.

The Child-man wept but gave no answer.

On the second gallows He saw the girl.
"My face is clean. You gave me both relationships
And friends . . . but only for an hour like this?"
The Child-man reached to her,
His eyes blinded by His pain.

On the third gallows was the
Man who owned His coat—
A coat now drenched in dying.
"Was My coat warm?" the Child-man probed.

"What is warm, Child-man?
Did You but make me warm
To face the chill of death?
We're all dying, can't You see?
All You did for us was temporary.
All Your gifts were but for our little needs.

Now we face the terror from which no one is ever
    free!
Do You not care!
We're dying . . . dying . . . dying!"

His hanging lovers all watched as He hobbled
To the center of their triple dying.
He climbed upon an empty gallows, hanged
    Himself
Until His hands and feet bore all their wounds.
Then His head collapsed
Toward the earth.
Their dying eased . . . *their* ropes came free,
Their hands and feet could move again
And they climbed down.

The Child-man smiled.
His final, precious words
Soared somehow sonnet-like:
"I am Love, made warm by nakedness.
I am Hope, made beautiful by craving ugliness!
I am Liberty, made swift by beggar's crutches!
I am Life that makes alive by dying."

Alive and free the trio walked away,
And passed a woman struggling up the hill
But paid her no attention as she climbed.
Soon she stood alone beneath the center gallows.
Her hood fell back.
The dying Child-man looked.
Their eyes met.
"I was afraid you'd come," He said.

"O Son, was the planet worth all this?"
She gestured to His hanging form.
"Should love bleed out its last for worlds
Too self-concerned to pity all its whispers
When it has lost the volume of its voice?

You loved but have no lovers.
Where are all those for whom this price is paid?"

His tears fell down to see her hurt.
Her tears fell too.
Their weeping birthed a river
Mighty in its grace.

Imperius awoke!
His face was wet!
He cried unto dark, more dark than even that
Which he had known when Emma left him,
"Should love in any world know such a fate?
Oh, glorious is this Child that I await."

Hate is bread—baked slowly
In the oven of our narcissism
And eaten with such haste
That we devour our hands,
And never notice till
We reach to touch what we adore
And find our fingers gone.

XVII

The desert sun streamed
Through the window of his
Shop at midday and
Ignited fragrant odors
From the sweet new cedar chips
That covered all the floor.
The fiend who dogged his doubts
Formed in a shaded corner
And sneered an unwelcome greeting.

"Hello, Artisan!"

The Artisan grimaced but said nothing.

"Your Trouvere is with child . . ."
The demonic voice went on,
"My child, not yours, poor unwise lover.
Will you not now call your Trouvere what she is?"

"Liar!"
Was all the Artisan could say.

"You called me liar before and found me true."

"I found your cloak beside her door.
I found my own mind subject
To discrepancies that you suggested."

"Bid the blindness in your love
Be healed.
Call hate, hate.
It is your maid who lies, not me."

"She cannot be with child.
She loves me
With a love that I return.

I see her smile, gentle as a desert rain,
In every sunrise."

"Give me no poetry
That sweetly closes both its eyes
While the unborn Child she carries,
Makes mockery of all your pretty words."

"Never!" cried the Artisan.
"I will not doubt my love's fidelity.
Doubt never cheapens love, it cheapens me.
But leave me, man . . .
I'm going now to see Trouvere.
Perhaps the months apart
Will soften our togetherness
And love will live as once it did.
But whether it live or no
She shall give answer to my doubts
And I will try your accusations
At the source of truth."

The Artisan left Trouvere's accuser.
Saying nothing else he journeyed to her
        home.
Still in his mind he wondered,
"Can Trouvere give any answers
When my very questions kill all trust?
Still, I'll ask them so I may sleep again."

Finally, he neared her simple dwelling!
She watched as he approached.

He knocked!
Trembling uncertainty at his appearance
Could not prevent her wild exuberance.
She flung the door wide.
"Artisan!" she cried,
And threw herself into happy arms

That closed about her.
His embrace seemed to say,
"Whatever is untold . . .
Whatever is withheld,
Whatever I believe or disbelieve
For this one moment of our lives, we touch,
And touching is the prize of lovers."

"They made the moment last
So that the aching weeks
That had separated them
Lost all their force.
They spoke in whispered syllables
Soft enough to heal
The hurt in all that must be said.
"Trouvere," the Artisan began,
"I know a man. And yet I don't.
He stalks me in the darkest fissures
Of my doubt.
He tells me things so damnable and dank
My heart can scarcely give them space."

"What sort of man?
What sort of things?" she asked.

"Don't think me mad, but pity me.
He says he is your lover!"

Trouvere turned away
And then turned back.
Tears stood silent in her eyes!
The Artisan felt so ashamed.
"Forgive me, dear Trouvere. I know not what to say.
But hear it all and then release my mind.
Each time he comes he says—
O forgive this blasphemy—
That you are with child—his child!"

Trouvere could bear his words no more.
She broke in weeping.
The Artisan drew her close
Begging, "Forgive me! O forgive, forgive!"
For a long while neither of them said anything.

"Artisan," she said at last.
"I too have had a visitor.
He springs from nothingness
And fills my mind with truths so overwhelming
That I scarcely can receive them all.
He told me I would have a child and—"
She stopped, knowing that
Her words defied all credibility.

"Trouvere, please . . ." he choked,
"Let's live with open hearts,
And lay it all in sun,
For nothing honest lives in shadows."

Painfully she turned her face toward him.
"He told me I would have a Child
And He would be Earthmaker's Son!"
"And you believed?"
The Artisan's voice rose to shouting level
That spoke the volume
Of his rising doubts.

"Please," Trouvere interrupted,
"You said let's lay it in the sun.
You must believe, for if you don't
I have no hope in all this world
That I shall ever be believed by anyone!
Whatever your strange visitor has told you,
He has lied!
I've never known nor yet desired another man.
But I must tell you

What I can hide no longer,
I AM WITH CHILD . . ."

The words were crushing stones.
He shook convulsively
And turned his face against the wall.

At last he turned again to her.
"Trouvere, I've never doubted anything you said.
But always in the past
I found some logic in your love.
You are for me this night
Life's great unhappiness.
If great Earthmaker be
And if He be pure love,
He would not, could not, violate
His own longstanding rules
Of nature and morality."

She broke again into tears.

He stood. She clung to him.
He pushed her back and turned,
"I'm going now, Trouvere.
While every value I have ever cherished dies.
The day has fled and left me only night.
The love is dark that once I blessed as light."

"God," I cried, "I need You,
Can You hear me? Are You there?"
The great glass throne seemed empty.
There was no one in His chair.
I waited in His absence.
Finally on my bloody knees
I laid my doubting obscene head
On His high-gilded guillotine,
And meekly said, "I trust!"

XVIII

$\mathcal{A}$s leaden days marched on
The crust of numbness
'Round her heart gave way.

Her singing joy subsided.
Earthmaker seemed both deaf and far away.
Ansond came not.
She made her way one noontime to the well
In the condemning light of midday.
Two women watched her making her approach
And scrutinized her, sizing her
Against some conversation
That had already passed with the other women
Of the village who had measured
Trouvere's aloofness and the reasons for it.
An older woman approached, took her hand,
Pried open Trouvere's fingers,
And dropped into her upturned palm
A stone of shining black.
Then folding Trouvere's slender hand
Around the stone of condemnation
Walked away.

Trouvere shuddered.
Soon, now, she would be dragged
Into the village center
To face a world of friends
Made alien by her obedience to
Demands they could not understand.
She sat down sighing in her loneliness.
"Will no one believe me!"

"I believe you!" Said a handsome man
Who settled next to her.
"At least I want to,
But consider this:

Is it possible that in some moment
Your mind has hidden from yourself
You slept with someone . . .
Your Artisan . . . or some soldier
From the garrison nearby?
They say these foreign devils
Have hypnotic charms that drug
All those that they seduce
Forbidding remembrance
Of their every full consent.
And so you sinned and yet you didn't.
Some dread narcotic enemy
Stole chastity and left you sinned against."

Her heart resisted!
"No!" She hesitated.
"Ansond told me I would bear a Son."

"Ansond!" He interrupted!
"O Trouvere,
He's the very sort of hypnotist
That I was speaking of.
Ansond has left a field of spoiled lovers
Maimed by his hypnosis.
And did he tell you too,
That you were specially favored?"

Trouvere felt ashamed.
"Yes, those were his words!"

"Would Earthmaker give you shame
Or call such visitors His friend?"

"But I saw a towering light
Falling in cascades of incandescence."

"Poor girl. So naive! So innocent!
Light and incandescence

Are but explosions of raw lust.
Seduction makes its own starbursts
Then names them after God.
Which cults are popular
That do not feed desire?
They each one teach us
That their lusty lights have come from the
      Almighty.
Which pagan temples
Do not think their passions pure?
Which cultic prostitutes
Do not believe they do great service?
Every profane bed
Boasts some loving chastity.
Your lights were bright deceptions.
But do not call your dark hallucinations, honest
      visions.
You were the naive pawn of great hypnotic power!"

She buried her head in her hands,
And then looked up to find him gone.
She felt her soul locked in a vise
Beyond all possibility of liberation.
"Earthmaker, give me a song
That I may give it back to You.

"Send soon the gentle rain and kiss
The parched philosophies of earth.
And wash my shabby rags of trust
And clothe me with a new cleansed worth.

"Immaculate in nature come
Swab dying from my dead hereafter.
Cut healing into stabbing woe
And bind my pain with laughter.

"Send soon the gentle rain. Rich dress
The desert night with wedding flowers

And run anemones into
A bridal quilt with tender showers.

"You, Father, I adore—for You
Alone can make my madness sane.
Embrace my need or I must die.
Great Sovereign, send Your gentle rain."

Lust in final form spends everything
To purchase headstones.
All passions die in graveyards.

XIX

The serpent came at sunset,
Black as the night that beckons death.

"I know you, fiend!"
The Artisan cried.
"Night made you rank,
As that dank canyon of the damned
Where you, no doubt,
Keep your hellish nest."

"Poor Artisan, you were deceived!
Your love now stumbles through the desert,
Weeping in her childish pain.
Alone in her naiveté,
Such a pity! Such a glory!
So easily deceived, so easily confused.
And you're so like her, man!
Whose child does Trouvere carry, Artisan?"

"I cannot say, but, now, at last
I know it isn't yours.
Nor have *you* ever entered
Into my domain of promise.
Nobility is smudged so easily in fallen worlds.
My poor Trouvere but lost her way
In some betraying moment
Where innocence could be abused."

"Don't justify her infidelity and call it love.
I stung her to unconsciousness,
And in my powerful and seducing form
I lay with her."
The great snake hissed and rose,
Lowered, throwing back his head
As though he'd thrust it forward in a strike.
The craftsman grabbed a heavy wedge of wood

And cried aloud,
"Come, you ugly terror!"

The hooded head swayed forward!
The hard black lips
Wrinkled backward into a hideous smile.
And while the cobra did not laugh,
Laughter—fiendish, hellish—
Broke in the air about them
As he slithered from the room.

The Artisan was now alone.
"O Trouvere, wherever are you now?" he cried.
"I need your touch and two mere words to live—
Give back my soul and whisper, 'I forgive'!"

I never have believed that love is blind
And yet, I know it does see best at night.

XX

The Artisan now knew that he must find
    Trouvere.
Nor could he wait for morning.
Driven by his need for her
He moved across the desert.
Even as he walked
His loneliness diminished.
While no one visible was there,
A set of footprints fell beside his own,
Blazing shadowy depressions in the starlit sand.

Gradually the unseen traveler materialized and
    spoke:
"Artisan, Trouvere's unborn Child
Will be Earthmaker's Son!"
The words were out at once.

"No!" The Artisan replied.
"That is Trouvere's tale,
But too preposterous.
Even if such a thing were possible
Earthmaker is too kind and loving
To lay such weight on her."

"Burdens have a way
Of being heavy in every world.
Do you suppose that only humans cry?
All that crushes human spirit
Also leaves the heart
Of Universal Spirit in a vise."

The Artisan said nothing.

"Earthmaker's burden
Now passes on to you.
You, Artisan, like your Trouvere, are chosen.

And from the double weight of His favor
Earthmaker's Troubadour shall come.
Marry Trouvere and protect her,
Knowing that the Child she soon brings forth
Is not your Child.
But you were born to be the Artisan Protector.
Serve the Father Spirit
By waiting with Trouvere until the Child is here.
And remember this,
All that makes you grieve today
Will in tomorrow's world break forth as song."

So saying Ansond vanished.
The Artisan was left alone
With that slow and certain light
That issues from a new-lit soul.
He knew that in the darkness out ahead
Awaited life and his Trouvere.
And he felt lighter than he had in years,
His heaviness all washed away by tears.

When lovers meet
On wounded feet
They hurt but
Find their aching sweet.

XXI

Trouvere rose quickly—her body large with life.
She studied the night sands
That stretched in tones of mottled brown
Unto the sky-lipped desert edge.
Her eyes greeted a distant shadow.

Trouvere studied a lonely form far out against the
    sand.
Until her eyes could comprehend the joyous truth,
"My Artisan, you've come!"

She threw open the door.
Her feet kept faith with what she saw.
She ran to him!

His searching eyes had seen her too.
His leaden steps found stamina!
With hearts, so long estranged
Compulsively they contemplated joy,
Then flew toward each other's arms.

"Trouvere . . ." was all he said.
The word was signal to their need.
They met . . . a blur of grand encirclement.

A lion roared! His presence blessed
The lovers' new communion.

It was a night when many journeys ended.
Later that same night
Melek also heard the lion roar!
Imperius, too!
That night, at last, the old ones met.

The beast's voice like a living trumpet
Called them both together, certain in their
    purposes

And yet uncertain why their
Odysseys had ended
At a common time and place.

"I'm Melek," said the old king.
"And I Imperius," the plague-survivor said.
The lion wandered off
And left the two sojourners
Face to face in starlight.
After silence Imperius asked at last,
"You've seen the Child?"
"I have," replied the king.
"I've seen Him twice before and seek Him even now,
To lay before Him my old coronet—
The single legacy of my decaying realm—
A crown befitting a far better Kingdom."

"I've nothing for Him," said Imperius,
"Except a blessing.
But bless this Child, I shall.
For every night is preface to some light
Each tyranny will yield at last to right."

In self-defense
The infant Hercules once strangled
   snakes around his cradle.
But motherhood defends her cradle with
Hands made iron by love
To save a life
More worthy than her own.

XXII

Trouvere knew the time had come.
She snuggled to her Artisan
And felt his warmth.
But the warmth was not for long.
A chill passed through their tiny dwelling,
The blast of icy air awakened her.
"He's here!"

Her Artisan woke with a start.
He too felt the coldness in the air.

"Trouvere, stay here,"
He whispered as he rose
And stood on the cold floor.
Her hand reached out for his
And pulled him back.
"I'll go," she whispered firmly.

She stood and sifted darkness
With her eyes.
"Where is he?" The craftsman asked.

"We have only to ask what would be
His greatest slur," she replied.
Their eyes both turned at once toward the cradle
Where a dingy luminescence issued forth.

Trouvere and her Artisan both knew
The ugly source of blighted light.
"Are you afraid?" The Artisan asked.

"Yes, she is afraid," an evil laughter emanated
From the center of the thin light.

Trouvere, steeled with purpose,
Crossed the earthen floor

And thrust her hand into the sickly light.
She clutched the scaly head, so large and flat
Her hand could barely grasp it.
With strength she did not know she had,
She drew the heavy thing of hate
With a lashing, writhing motion
Out into the room.
She hurled the heavy body to the floor
And with her bare foot crushed the ugly reptile's
    head.
It was over in an instant, that left her marveling
That she had dared to do it.
Still the yellow glare was gone
And triumphant starlight sifted through the
    windows,
And fell upon the long, still form.

The Artisan now lit a lamp and in the better light
They both beheld the fiend's forbidding size.
Only then did Trouvere start to tremble,
For in the light, her courage seemed much poorer
Than the richness of her deed.

The snake was dead!
The room was somehow warmer.
The craftsman lifted up the lifeless thing,
Resolved to take it so far away that Trouvere
Would never have to look at it again.
He bore his evil burden out into the night.
But as he carried it, it grew lighter.
At first he thought that he imagined it,
But in a while knew that it was true.
In fifty steps across the desert
The serpent's form was fading
Even as the weight grew lighter.
In but a few steps more the snake was gone.
The Artisan now carried nothing,
And as the dead thing vanished in his hands,

He saw a hooded man running off into the night.
He shuddered at the strange event,
Chilled of soul and terrified by the knowledge
That Hell yet stalked the world.
Disappointed that the monster lived, he turned
And made his way back to the house.

"He is not dead, is he?" Trouvere guessed.

"No," said the Artisan,
"Still he has tasted our resolve
And he knows that we are settled in our
        commitment to the Father Spirit.
He nevermore shall make us sleep in fear.
For he only dares to raise his fanged face
Against those souls
Who live without a sense of who they are."
He paused a moment and then said suddenly,
"Trouvere . . . you acted with such strong
        resolve . . .
A mother's instinct?"

"Perhaps!
But more than that, I know
Our Son must one day face his hideous, hissing
        form.
Somehow, ahead of time I acted
As example for our unborn Son,
That evil cannot stand if good is unafraid."

The Artisan drew Trouvere close.
"Strength is the crown of queens who face their
        fears
And courage steels the eye, forbidding tears."

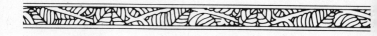

No shot was ever heard around the
    world.
In fact, in all of human history
Only two sounds have been heard
    around the entire world . . .
The first:
A newborn baby's cry, saying, "It is
    begun."
The second:
A young man's dying cry, saying,
    "It is finished."

XXIII

A knock fell firmly, gently on the door.
The Artisan opened it
With only sand and starlight answering.
Then suddenly, like an apparition
An old woman appeared,
"I am Gerain,
I know not how to tell you why I am here.
I woke as one who slept for centuries
Then came awake, called to redeem my very life
By being midwife to the purposes of God.
I tell you I am mad with mystery.
A lion roared and woke me, I followed, and . . ."

"Say no more," the Artisan reached out.

"See the heavens," the old woman's skyward gaze
        turned every face.
"Behold the stars that form the constellation of the
        lion
Have aligned themselves
Like stellar soldiers in an honor guard."

"How can this be?" Trouvere inquired.
Gerain, the old one, spoke low.
"The children in the mountains say
That when the Troubadour
Has come to sing His song,
The very stars will be as stepping stones
Between eternal realms."

Trouvere felt the Baby move within her.

Pain sometimes needs a silent witness.
And so Gerain said nothing else
But worked in quiet tenderness
While Trouvere's Artisan stood praying

As a sentinel might pray,
Looking through the very walls
As if some icon of Earthmaker was
Emblazoned past the ceiling in images
That held themselves from every eye
But his.
Trouvere knew pain but
Never once cried out.
At that small space where
The deepness of the night begins to fade
And the timid morning
Has not as yet declared itself
A Baby cried.

"There are two men at the door,"
The Artisan called through his joy.
Gerain opened the door and admitted
Melek and Imperius,
Who entered the small house reluctantly.
For there was in that room a sweet forbidding
    sanctity
That seemed to hold them back.
But Trouvere's demeanor put them so at ease
They overcame their hesitance
And pushed on in to see the Baby.

"Convergence comes," said Melek,
"The stars align themselves,
This Child is He
Whom every world has sung."

Trouvere sat upright in her bed
And in spite of every instinct
Given her by instant motherhood
She handed old Imperius her Child.

He took the Baby!
Tears came! Yet he looked past the Child,

As though his eye had focused somewhere past
    the candle flame
And fallen on his beloved,
Waiting in another world.

"Emma," he breathed, "I hold the earnest of our
    promise in my hands.
This child shall pave the way between
Our realms. The plague has fled,
And death itself is dead.
The dawn of hope is here.
Awake, ten thousand galaxies!
Polaris, bow your head! And Vega! Betelgeuse!
The vast Earthmaker, cosmic in His Grace,
Has locked Himself within a little space.
Behold, He whimpers weakly in a world
He made in strength. He who owns all lands
Is now reduced to poverty. He cannot walk
Who strode the galaxies. His tiny hands
Once light-years wide, are chubby-fingered now.
His dying world was weeping in the night.
He would not let it languish without light!
You sluggish quasars cease your cosmic flight
And listen! Here is a symphony of worth.
Oh, you proud skies, kneel down and kiss the
    earth!"

Imperius stopped his psalm and held the Child
Close to the candle fire.
He spoke again but not unto the Child,
"O Emma,
Come catch the glory etched in candlelight.
All universal being has, this night,
Broken forth in long-awaited rhapsody,
A maiden's song has spawned a symphony."

He left off speaking to his Emma
And kissed the Child.

He then began again,
"I once scorned ev'ry fearful thought of death,
When it was but the end of pulse and breath,
But now my eyes have seen that past the pain
There is a world that's waiting to be claimed.
Earthmaker, Holy, let me now depart,
For living's such a temporary art.
And dying is but getting dressed for God,
Our graves are merely doorways cut in sod."

It is faith that lights the eye—
Not reason!

XXIV

When He was old enough to walk
Trouvere brought the
Child back to the desert.
He grew, well nurtured by her love.
She told Him of His coming often
But only when He slept.
She sang to Him of love and mystery
As lullabies to keep her memories alive.

One balmy summer eve she left her Artisan alone
And carried her Son asleep within her arms
To that same desert edge
Where He had been conceived
And smiling down upon her sleeping Son she
        said,
"I met You here before I gave You birth.
There was a lion in our world then,
I haven't seen him since You came.
Old Melek, too, has left our world
Returning to his kingdom.
Our very lives are testament to his great gift.
We spent his crown for bread."

She hushed her whispered words
And traded them for a magnificat
Which bathed her sleeping Son
With a richness amplified by desert breezes.

"Did ever earth hold dreams more mad than
        mine!
That I, a desert dweller, should become
The intersection of two realms of time,
And strike the empty, sluggish ages dumb.
How shall I sing and what? Or should I sing
At all? It is too excellent for me.
If I had hushed my inner symphonies,

His music would have burst from rocks
 and trees."

"O come with me, poor world of songless men.
A storm of love has gathered in the sky
Above your heads! It shall not come again!
Run to the center of the storm: there lie!
For there at reason's edge all glory lies.
Nay, lies no longer now, but reaching comes,
Treading down the unbelieving skies,
Crushing distant ice and dying suns.

"Stare outward, starward—far as vision may.
Where eye at last meets dim capacity
And lifting night folds into dark'ning day
And stars flee from their erring galaxies.
Can spirit live in flesh? Can all that is
Not touchable be touched . . . the silent rhyme
Be heard . . . the hidden ever seen? Yes! His
Vast timelessness falls now in love with time.

"Despair at last has felt the heel of light
For love has come and plans to spend the night."

A lion roared!

The sound seemed faint and far away
Like Melek's aging kingdom.
It was the last time Trouvere ever heard the beast
And yet his roarings never grew so faint
Their glad reverberations ceased to echo in her
 heart.
The villagers told tales
Of a great lion that sometimes slept
Upon the grave of old Imperius,
Who had gone to join his Emma
Soon after he had held the promised Child.
Trouvere never doubted

That their reunion made the heavens
Sweeter than they might have been.

The seasons of all visions lose themselves
At last in ordinary years,
And in the passing of those years
The Child grew up in common ways
And all things seemed more ordinary.
And yet Trouvere could tell the age was different.
A strange, dim melody nightly came
And floated to the desert floor to kiss the sand,
As though the world had come to love itself.
Oftentimes Trouvere could hear the music
Faint and nearly voiceless. Hauntingly
It begged her wait until the Child grew.
She knew that when the Child was grown
The lion would be back and when he roared
A kingless world would welcome its new Lord.